Wanton Thoughts

MUKTA ARYA

PARTRIDGE

A Penguin Random House Company

To order additional copies of this book, contact
Toll Free 800 101 2657 (Singapore)
Toll Free 1 800 81 7340 (Malaysia)
orders.singapore@partridgepublishing.com

www.partridgepublishing.com/singapore

This collection of poems is dedicated

To,

my father Mr. Laxmi Narain,
and,
my mother Dr.(Mrs) Manju Garg,
who let my imagination soar and helped expand my horizon,
and supported all my initiatives . . .

To,
my sister Dr. Prerna Arya,
my brother Neeraj Arya,
my nephew Ankit Arya,
and my sister-in-law Geet Rathi,
for being my real and invaluable friends,
in addition to being my family . . .

To,
my friends (Harsh Arora, Zehera Mecklai, Aditi Puri,
Firdaus Padamsee and Farida Padamsee),
some of my dear colleagues and mentors at work,
and especially Karen Khaw,
who encourages me to try new things,
and who is responsible for the publication of this book.

This collection of poems, like the title "Wanton Thoughts"
is just that. Thoughts that arose on the spur of the moment,
thoughts that are here, there and everywhere, stimulated by life
and incidents around me.

Hence, the poems are no particular order—they are
a sprinkling of thoughts.

Life

The following poems are based on deeper meaning of life, thoughts about "being" and a lot of introspection.

I think . . .

I think of the steps with spring,
I think of the lightness of being,
I think of the shrinking chasm,
Between reality and my dream . . .

I think of birds that tweet,
I think of eyes that meet,
I think of the sweet aroma,
That covers the panorama . . .

I think of flowers in May,
I think of trees that sway,
I think of bold colour,
That envelopes with valour . . .

A matter of time . . .

I walk on cold steps in the morning,
air cutting through my strides . . .
A dead silence at each turning,
broken by fragment of tides . . .

I wonder how it is so chilled,
when in the night it was festive . . .
The same silence was filled,
with crowds that were restive . . .

A voice told me with a calm tone
it's just a matter of time . . .
A piece of metal, wood and bone
may become a melodious chime . . .

If there's sunshine . . .

Every day is a new day,
With events that cross the way,
Dragon that they may slay,
Keeping sorrows at bay.

Every day is a new day,
With life affected by a simple nay,
I look at it and say,
If there's sunshine, make hay.

Freedom

Freedom is what makes life exciting,
Restless thoughts are so interesting,
Excitement of the journey is intoxicating,
End is not actually that stimulating,
Determined for life to be exhilarating,
Out-of-the-box thinking is captivating,
My life with freedom is really fascinating!

I wade through life . . .

I wade through life,
With wonders at every corner,
A twinkle in my eye,
And a feeling quite tender.

I wade through life,
Unravelling the little mysteries,
Joy at every step,
To discover new territories.

I wade through life,
And meet people so warm,
Love getting lost in conversations,
With such abundant charm.

Differences

A lot of difference,
Between folks,
Is not by chance,
And is not idle talk.

It's a matter,
Of preferences,
And the latter,
Equals differences.

The variety,
Is the excitement,
Adding to gaiety,
And enjoyment.

The disparity,
Is the trigger,
For creativity,
And things bigger.

The Sands of Time . . .

Buried in the sands of time,
I thought of a life sublime,
An age that was a mime,
Of love in the prime.

Days that stretched long,
And hours that sang a song,
Lovely days when we got along,
And felt alone even in a throng.

A lot of indecision,
A sweet and sour tension,
Intense heated discussion,
And a very sensitive question.

I don't know if that's what I miss,
Something more or less a bliss,
I do definitely know this,
Without you, there's something amiss.

Sometimes

Sometimes I want to fly,
To a faraway place,
A land of slow pace,
And people with grace.

Sometimes I want to fly,
To a beautiful street,
Where people meet,
And is a visual treat.

Sometimes I want to fly,
To a barren land,
Pushed by a hand,
With a magic wand.

Sometimes I want to fly
To my inner world,
Veiled and twirled,
With desires curled.

Relief

Relief . . .

That's what I felt,
When I finally knew,
When I figured out,
My life-goal anew.

A direction,
A somewhat clear way,
No further dilly-dally,
And thoughts in a sway.

Expectations

Most of my life,
I didn't expect anything,
From anyone,
Except myself.

Life went on,
Nice and lovely,
Without tears,
Pain and anxiety.

I was surprised
Pleasantly,
When I got something
Unexpectedly.

It happened
A number of times,
I started expecting
More.

And
Guess what?
I was really
Disappointed.

So I am back
To my old
Non-expecting
Way of living,

And life is
Suddenly
Much
Better.

Uncertain

When the situation,
It's uncertain,
Neither this nor that,
Neither here nor there.

When the mind,
Looks this way,
And the heart,
The other way.

When one moment,
I crave the thrill,
And the next,
I want it real.

I don't know why,
But,
I am certain,
I love it.

But . . .

It's peaceful.
It's relaxed.
It's quiet.

But . . .

The calm is so stressed!

The stillness is so troubled!

The composure is so ruffled!

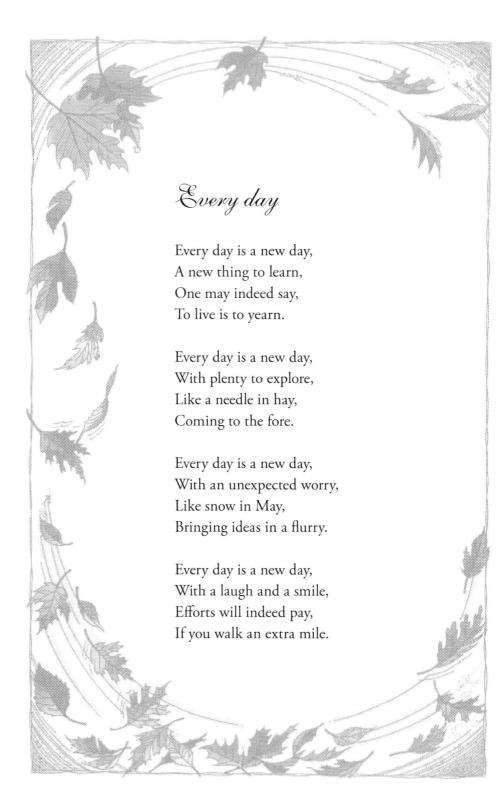

Every day

Every day is a new day,
A new thing to learn,
One may indeed say,
To live is to yearn.

Every day is a new day,
With plenty to explore,
Like a needle in hay,
Coming to the fore.

Every day is a new day,
With an unexpected worry,
Like snow in May,
Bringing ideas in a flurry.

Every day is a new day,
With a laugh and a smile,
Efforts will indeed pay,
If you walk an extra mile.

If you want . . .

A lot to do
If you want,
nothing at all,
If you think you can't!

The will power,
Is all from you,
Nobody will add,
An extra hue!

The ability,
To be happy,
Or the decision,
To be sad!

It's completely,
In your hands,
And is like,
A magic wand!

Is it?

Is it delight?
Is it romance?
Is it kind words?
Is it creation?

Or Is it ecstasy?

Is it what you like?
Is it what you want?
Is it what you need?
Is it beyond your reach?

Or Is it harmony?

Is it being alive?
Is it money?
Is it good food?
Is it being healthy?

Or is it sheer joy?

Is it birds?
Is it flowers?
Is it pleasure
Is it swaying trees?

Or is it a sigh of exhilaration?

Is happiness a part
Or a sum of
Everything?

Little things . . .

A laugh here,
A light there,
Meeting a friend,
Adopting a trend.

Writing a post,
Eating a toast,
Life looks pink,
With an exciting link.

A lot to see,
With the aroma of tea.

What a Day!

Crazy,
Hazy,
Lazy,
May Day,
A truly relaxed,
Lovely warm day,
To ponder on the dry,
Yellow hay.

Only Yours . . .

The height of happiness,
The depth of sadness,
The thrill of newness,
The joy of craziness . . .

The emotions,
That lead to dizziness,
Are only yours,
Clouding everything with,
A pleasant haziness . . .

Is it a sign?

An endless trail of leafless trees,
Showing to all and sundry,
A number of bird's nest,
They held close to their chest,
And hid so well during the good times . . .

Is it a sign that in adverse situations,
Things which blended and were ignored
Come to the fore,
Like an eye-sore,
To be picked and pointed at?

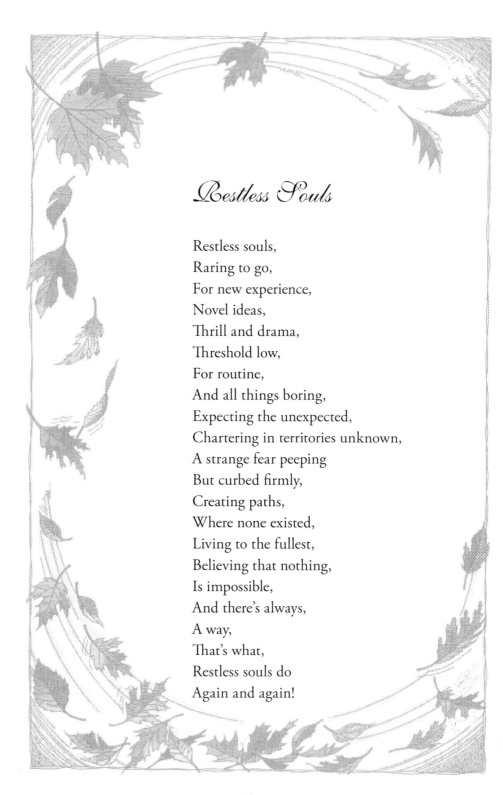

Restless Souls

Restless souls,
Raring to go,
For new experience,
Novel ideas,
Thrill and drama,
Threshold low,
For routine,
And all things boring,
Expecting the unexpected,
Chartering in territories unknown,
A strange fear peeping
But curbed firmly,
Creating paths,
Where none existed,
Living to the fullest,
Believing that nothing,
Is impossible,
And there's always,
A way,
That's what,
Restless souls do
Again and again!

A smile

Just a little smile,
And it can turn . . .
Strangers to friends
Tension to happiness
Issues to solutions
Questions to answers
Drudgery to fun
Chores to frolic
and . . . .
Life to love!

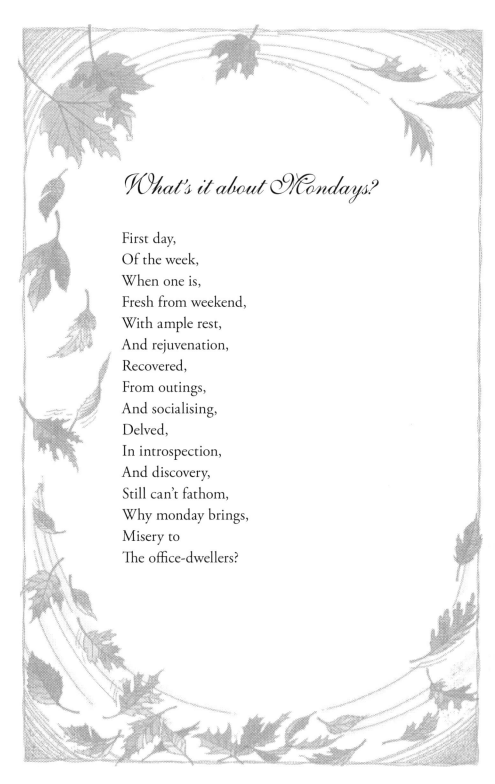

What's it about Mondays?

First day,
Of the week,
When one is,
Fresh from weekend,
With ample rest,
And rejuvenation,
Recovered,
From outings,
And socialising,
Delved,
In introspection,
And discovery,
Still can't fathom,
Why monday brings,
Misery to
The office-dwellers?

At the last moment . . .

When it's the last moment,
Life is actually a steep gradient,
Ideas suddenly come flowing,
For an impending meeting, which is very important.

The pressure of time,
And the credibility at stake,
Makes one come up with ways,
And solutions that are somewhat great.

The compression of time,
And a number of thoughts which collide,
Makes the last minute presentation,
One of the best the mind could provide.

Faith

Faith is when you know,
That you can pour your heart out,
And that it will still be between two of you . . .

Faith is when you don't even have to say something,
And he/she knows what you want exactly . . .
Faith is when you don't think twice about calling them,
Or land on their doorstep unannounced . . .

Faith cannot be measured,
Faith is just felt.

In numerous small ways,
And makes you feel,
There's someone whom you can trust,
Whenever there's a need . . . .

Together

It's so nice to be with family & friends
The warmth and the affection,
Makes you look at life,
With unadulterated admiration.

The meaningless jokes,
Revival of memories, funny and touching,
The pleasure of being together,
Makes a gesture, so completely moving.

The pleasure of reading a book . . .

Immersed in the world of words,
With characters alive and energetic,
The charm of reading a novel, lying on the bed,
Is bound to make ones mind very active!

A world created out of mind's eyes,
With thoughts weaving webs which are tangled,
Losing self in another world
Is something I will never trade
for things and ideas, new-fangled!

Trigger

Sitting at my desk,
Gazing vacantly at my laptop screen,
With unread e-mails piling up,
I wonder why our work makes us preen!

It's strange that some days are so busy,
One wonders, how one can even breathe,
And some days seem to linger on and on,
Wrapped with boredom, like a sheath!

Then, suddenly some word or action,
Bounces up from the screen,
And the lethargy and the boredom,
Flies out of the window . . . neat and clean!

Ideas come without warning,
And suddenly take some shape,
I spring back to life,
and immerse in life with a faster pace!

Life

Life without crests and troughs,
Life without joy and sorrow,
Life without highs of achievements,
Life without depths of despair,
Life without fun and frolic,
Life without things which are new,
Life without respect for others,
Life without responsibility that bothers,
Life without different colours,
Life without a little unpredictability,
Life without raindrops and blossoms,
Life without imagination,
Life without love and laughter,
Life without family and friends,
Life without something to claim as your own . . .
Life without all of the above is just . . . meaningless!

Love

The following poems show few facets of love . . .

Restless

In the midst of a crowd,
With plethora of action,
Mind is focused,
But eyes are wanton.

Wandering here and there,
With slight tension,
Waiting for a stolen glance,
Full of passion.

Days have gone by,
With marked absence,
The eyes are restless,
For a real connection.

Eyes

A sideways glance,
Lands you in a trance.

An ignored look,
Leaves you on a hook.

A simple hello,
And ice becomes mellow.

A prolonged gaze,
And you are in a haze.

A glimpse out of the blue,
Colours you with a hue.

Two hearts, it ties,
That's the power of the eyes.

A Quiet Smile

Sneaking from the corner of the mouth,
It manages to appear like a quiet smile,
It never comes out in the open,
But, has a meaning that stretches a mile.

Something that's covert and shyly hidden,
A wonderful, deep thought in that quiet smile,
Makes me feel really warm and fuzzy,
As, has a meaning that stretches a mile.

Still . . .

It's not tangible . . .
No commitment,
No promises,
No rosy future,
No strings,
No burden,
But still . . .
It just feels nice . . .
To be with,
Some special ones!

Places

Some places have a much deeper impact on us.
Discover some of the places and uniqueness of these places
through my eyes . . . Mumbai, Goa, South African Safari, Moscow,
St. Petersburg and my favourite-Typhoon No. 8 in Hong Kong . . .

Morning

It's 5:45 in the morning.

Raindrops are creating havoc,
Water puddles are dancing,
The trees are swaying,
Birds nowhere to be seen,
Cold wind attacks the face,
Watchmen everywhere are awake,
Some enthusiastic runners,
Are conquering the streets.

Few people are ready for work,
The mid-level escalator,
Has come to life,
And the life in pubs and bars,
Is completely dead.

The mind wants to walk fast,
The feet do not support.
It's just 5:45 in the morning.

Never a chance!

In a foreign land,
Though one is sometimes alone,
There's never a chance,
For one to be lonely.

The smiling faces,
The amazing decors,
The wonderful aromas,
The eccentricities of,
All places,
Big or small.

The varied music,
The melodious accents,
The curious glances,
The methods,
The madness,
The blossoms.

The winding roads,
The noise,
The fun,
The cackle,
The spirit,
And the vibrance.

How can one ever,
Feel lonely,
With life around,
Quite lovely?

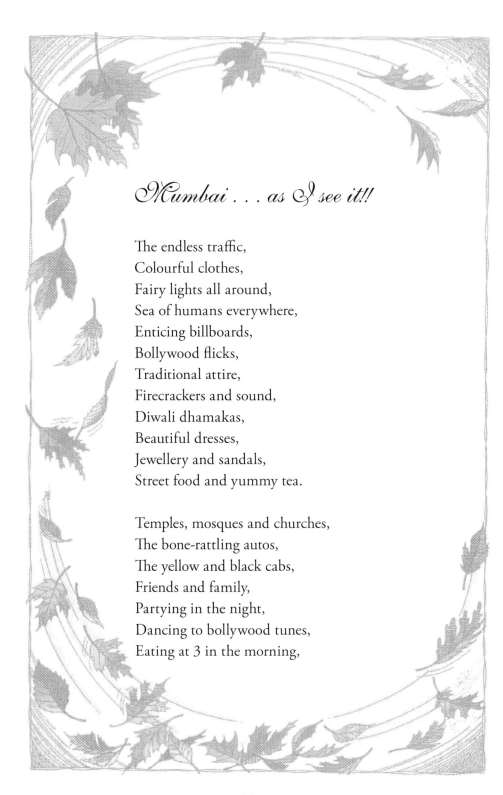

Mumbai . . . as I see it!!

The endless traffic,
Colourful clothes,
Fairy lights all around,
Sea of humans everywhere,
Enticing billboards,
Bollywood flicks,
Traditional attire,
Firecrackers and sound,
Diwali dhamakas,
Beautiful dresses,
Jewellery and sandals,
Street food and yummy tea.

Temples, mosques and churches,
The bone-rattling autos,
The yellow and black cabs,
Friends and family,
Partying in the night,
Dancing to bollywood tunes,
Eating at 3 in the morning,

Parathas and rajma,
Dal and chawal,
Sev puri and pani puri,
Upset tummy,
And pleasant fatigue.

Driving on familiar roads,
The memories of countless
Times, I trod on them,
The time when I learnt driving,
The small grocery shop,
My preferred petrol station,
My ex-gym,
The small joint for frankies,
Our parking lot,
The nooks and corners
Of wonderful Mumbai,
Avoiding the potholes,
And crashing into them,
FM radio and old hindi songs,

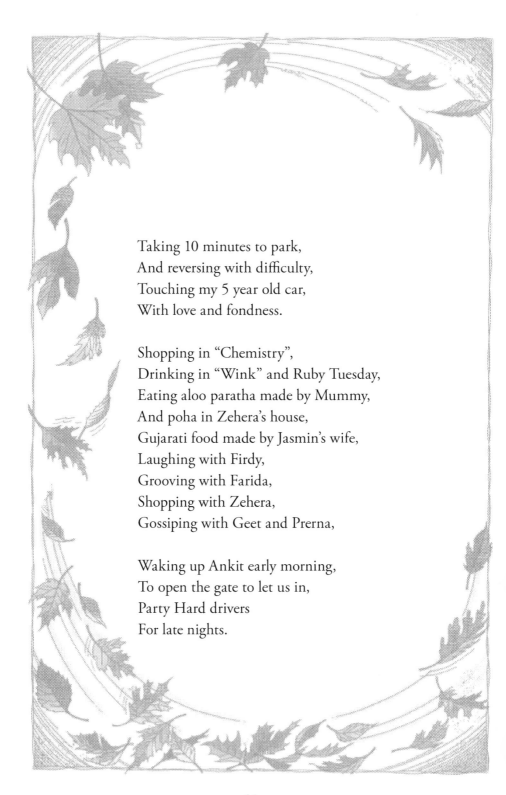

Taking 10 minutes to park,
And reversing with difficulty,
Touching my 5 year old car,
With love and fondness.

Shopping in "Chemistry",
Drinking in "Wink" and Ruby Tuesday,
Eating aloo paratha made by Mummy,
And poha in Zehera's house,
Gujarati food made by Jasmin's wife,
Laughing with Firdy,
Grooving with Farida,
Shopping with Zehera,
Gossiping with Geet and Prerna,

Waking up Ankit early morning,
To open the gate to let us in,
Party Hard drivers
For late nights.

Movies and vodka orange with Harsh,
Speeding across the sea-link,
With windows rolled down,
Meeting loved ones,
And reliving sweet memories,
Meeting Aditi and Muffi,
On their first wedding anniversary,
Being happy together,
Amongst a veil of smoke,
Hitting the hotspots,
And going back to old favourites.

Sleeping till late,
Having tea before opening the eyes,
Marine drive,
And worli sea-face,
Mumbai,
will never ever,
leave my heart!

Typhoon No. 8

Heard about it a number of times,
Read and warned about it . . .
A simple phenomenon
Called Typhoon No. 8,
And . . . one Thursday . . .
It was Typhoon No. 8 in HK . . .
A natural calamity hovering,
Right over our heads,
The winds were howling,
The seas were growling,
But strangely . . .
Most of us were happy,
To have an unexpected holiday,
To loll around in bed,
For just a few more hours,
And become a couch potato.

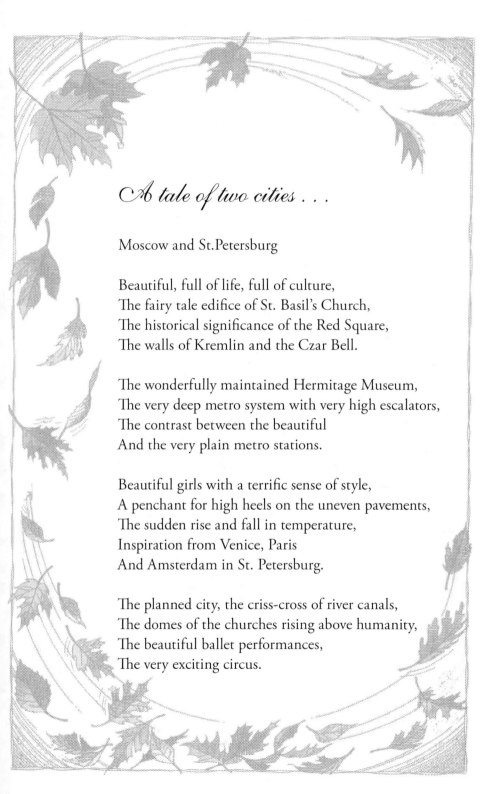

A tale of two cities . . .

Moscow and St.Petersburg

Beautiful, full of life, full of culture,
The fairy tale edifice of St. Basil's Church,
The historical significance of the Red Square,
The walls of Kremlin and the Czar Bell.

The wonderfully maintained Hermitage Museum,
The very deep metro system with very high escalators,
The contrast between the beautiful
And the very plain metro stations.

Beautiful girls with a terrific sense of style,
A penchant for high heels on the uneven pavements,
The sudden rise and fall in temperature,
Inspiration from Venice, Paris
And Amsterdam in St. Petersburg.

The planned city, the criss-cross of river canals,
The domes of the churches rising above humanity,
The beautiful ballet performances,
The very exciting circus.

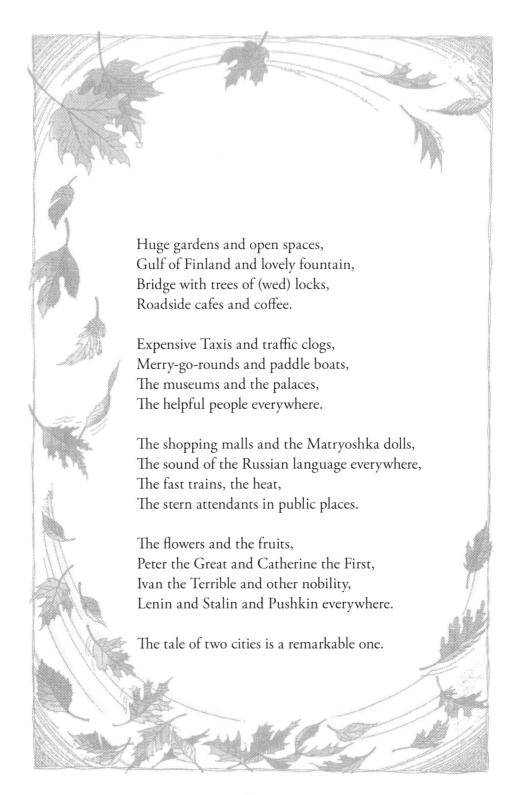

Huge gardens and open spaces,
Gulf of Finland and lovely fountain,
Bridge with trees of (wed) locks,
Roadside cafes and coffee.

Expensive Taxis and traffic clogs,
Merry-go-rounds and paddle boats,
The museums and the palaces,
The helpful people everywhere.

The shopping malls and the Matryoshka dolls,
The sound of the Russian language everywhere,
The fast trains, the heat,
The stern attendants in public places.

The flowers and the fruits,
Peter the Great and Catherine the First,
Ivan the Terrible and other nobility,
Lenin and Stalin and Pushkin everywhere.

The tale of two cities is a remarkable one.

A lone tree . . .

A lone tall tree,
Was found standing,
All by itself,
On a mound,
Swaying with the breeze,
Sunlight fading away,
With an attitude meek,
The golden aura,
And the crimson streak . . .
The flowers blossoming,
At it's feet,
And the birds stopping by,
For a tweet . . .

You all know me as a wild buck . . .

a little jump
heart got a thump . . .

marvelling at the beauty
of nature's bounty . . .

hiding and peeking
looking and seeking . . .

enemies and fiends
and some loyal friends . . .

life is interesting
with pecks and stings . . .

with me is good luck
you all know me, a "wild buck" . . .

A morning in Goa

A splash, a dash of colours,
on the gray road.

A tinge, a splatter of flowers,
and a jumping toad.

A varied splosh of green,
on a cloudy day.

A time for fauna to preen,
with a lot to say.

A flurry of curly waves,
on pristine sand.

A stillness that caves,
completely unplanned.

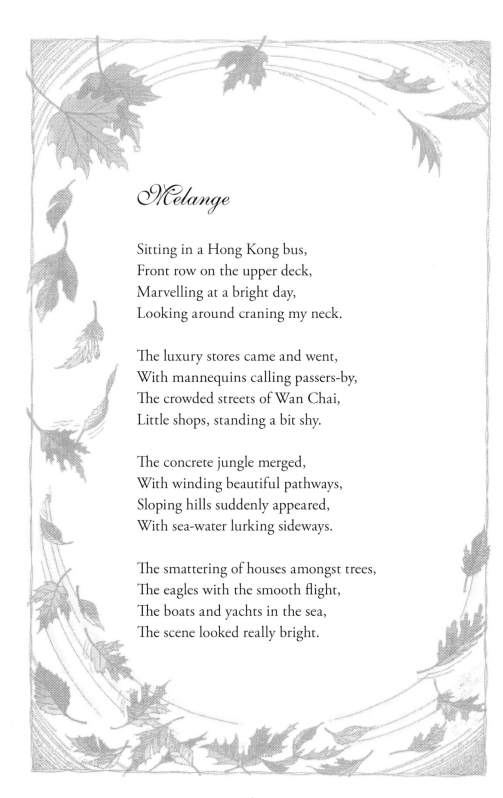

Melange

Sitting in a Hong Kong bus,
Front row on the upper deck,
Marvelling at a bright day,
Looking around craning my neck.

The luxury stores came and went,
With mannequins calling passers-by,
The crowded streets of Wan Chai,
Little shops, standing a bit shy.

The concrete jungle merged,
With winding beautiful pathways,
Sloping hills suddenly appeared,
With sea-water lurking sideways.

The smattering of houses amongst trees,
The eagles with the smooth flight,
The boats and yachts in the sea,
The scene looked really bright.

The cool calm waters of the sea,
The shore coloured in peach,
The families huddled together,
Enjoying barbecue on the beach.

A melange of nature and concrete,
Ambition, crowd and tranquillity,
That's how I see Hong Kong,
Co-existing with harmony.

Only . . . in the world of holidays

Away from the busy days,
The hustle,
The bustle,
The daily grind,
The duties,
The rights,
Only in the world of holidays,
We mortals,
Find out,
Our real calling,
The strengths,
The fears,
The desires,
The likings,
The passion,
The ability,
To take on the world,
Only and only . . .
In the world of holidays.